The Writer's Tracker

For Work, Income, Expenses, & Taxes

the Serious Writer's Business Ledger

____

Tax Year

Scribes & Scribblers Publishing

Serious Writing Tools for Serious Writers

The Writer's Tracker for Work, Income Expenses, & Taxes

ISBN: 978-1-961502-14-7

Cover created on Canva and BookBrush.
Graphics and fonts from Canva and Deposit Photos.

12621 N Tatum Blvd #1782 Phoenix, AZ 85032

esmagill@esmagillauthorshop.com

www.esmagillauthorshop.com
www.scribesandscribblerspub.com

Contents

Writing as Your Professional Business

Introduction

Welcome, full-time and part-time and sometimes writers. Like many, you've dreamed of earning an income from your writing. And like many writers, you probably never expected all the accounting, paperwork, and taxes. If you see your writing as a money-making business, then don't let your status (full-time, part-time, or sometimes) keep you from the benefits of treating it like one.

I know a lot of writers, and I'm shocked at the number who don't claim their writing work deductions when they file their taxes. These are people I know who are making an honest go at making writing their livelihood. When I quiz them as to why they don't claim their writing deductions, they say things like "I don't make any money writing" or "I don't make enough money writing." I then ask if they spent money on their writing venture. Of course they did. Writing is a business, and like any business it can take several years before realizing a profit. So even if you're in the red, claim those deductions. If you're currently employed or receiving a pension, you can reduce your tax burden by claiming your writing expenses.

77% of authors surveyed identify as self-published, 17% as hybrid, with 5% traditional, notes Written Word Media.

With the rise of self-publishing, so much more is involved in getting your writing work out into the world. There are book formatting apps to purchase, like Atticus, Scrivener, Vellum. You will want to make graphics for your marketing campaigns – Canva and BookBrush. You'll also need editing software, such as ProWritingAid and AutoCrit. Collecting emails for your newsletter? Then you'll need something like Mailerlite. Direct sales are booming with authors now selling their books on their own websites, and with that comes a whole set of financial considerations. Think about all the things you need to invest in: marketing, promotions, book fairs, reams of paper, ink for your printer, bookmarks, writing courses, book signings, conventions. The list goes on and on. Being a writer requires a financial investment, and with that comes business and tax responsibilities.

Call it a tracker, ledger or workbook, it can do more than just record-keeping for taxes. This can be your writing business center:

- Keep track of all the writing apps you use, along with their costs, and whether those apps are a monthly or yearly or a lifetime subscription.
- Make notes on which apps are helpful and which you can unsubscribe from.
- Keep track of your queries and submissions, as well as applications for awards and grants.

- With its calendars, you can even use this tracker to plan your social media or newsletter campaigns.
- Use the calendars not just to track your work time but also to create a timeline for writing your next novel or creating your next project.

- Keep track of podcast interviews, book signings, convention panels, and more.
- It becomes a reference book. Use last year's information to run your writing business this year.

Disclaimer:

This tracker does not give any advice about taxes, business, or related topics.
This tracker is a ledger only. It consists of tables and directions.
Consult the IRS.
Use a professional accountant, lawyer, or tax advisor for all your tax and business needs.
This workbook is for the purpose of recording information only.

Do you do your accounting on a computer spreadsheet? Great! But do you know what to include in your spreadsheet? How familiar are you with all the deductions you might be able to claim? Did you know there are differences in how you can claim travel expenses if you're an employee versus if you're self-employed? Do you know how to claim auto expenses or your home office? Do you know how to complete a Schedule C? Use this Tracker as your spreadsheet guide.

Did you know that the IRS requires you to document your work hours and projects? If an audit pops up, you must satisfy the IRS's requirement that you be able to prove that writing is your business and not just a hobby.

Did you know your responsibility as a self-employed taxpayer is greater than that of an employee taxpayer on an employer's payroll? Yes, you read that correctly. This means you need to run your writing endeavor as a business. Keeping accurate records is paramount. Your writing

hours, submissions, published and unpublished work, expenses, and income all need to be documented. The upside to being self-employed is that you get to reap tax benefits that employees cannot.

Are you keeping thorough and accurate business records? *The Writer's Tracker for Work, Income, Expenses, & Taxes* is designed for accounting your work hours, your projects, your writing income, and your expenses. There's even a Schedule C included so you can organize your taxes. When you file your taxes, it is important to have accurate records and accounting for your writing business — digital or paper, or both.

Remember: consult a tax professional for your tax needs. This workbook does not provide tax advice or business information. This is an accounting ledger which contains only tables and forms.

According to Written Word Media's 2025 Indie Author Survey: Those in the $1,000+ per month **group almost always have: More books (often** 10+, **and very often** series**);**
An active email list; **A mindset:** "This is a business."

The IRS and Taxes

The best advice is visit **www.irs.gov** for your tax needs. When it comes to running a business, there are so many rules, laws, guidelines, regulations, and forms. Plus, tax law is always changing — from year to year but also within the current year.

DO YOUR RESEARCH AND GET EXPERT AND PROFESSIONAL ADVICE.

Be aware of your tax year and the publication date of any resource you consult. IRS updates to documents and Web pages may not be available at the time of this tracker's publication. Find the resources for your tax year.

A Word on Sales Tax (U.S.)

When selling goods (real or digital), sales tax must be considered.
Sales tax laws and requirements are very complex and vary from state to state and even within a state. It is your responsibility to understand the laws. Consult a Tax Professional.
Here is a good resource: https://stripe.com/guides/how-to-file-sales-tax-us

***Note: Sales tax you collect and remit directly to a state is deductible from your Gross Income.**
***Sales tax remitted by a platform on your behalf is NOT deductible.**

HOMEWORK

Really!
What is NEXUS in relation to sales tax in the United States?

A word on Sales Tax (U.S.) or VAT (European Union) or any other tax on goods:

Some publishing and payment platforms do not remit sales tax (including VAT or other tax on goods) on your behalf. It is your responsibility to understand the laws and requirements nationally and internationally. Consult a Tax Professional.

Hobby or Business

The IRS has rules about what constitutes a business and a hobby. Here is the website: https://www.irs.gov/newsroom/hobby-or-business-heres-what-to-know-about-that-side-hustle. According to the IRS, here are 9 ways they use to determine if your venture is just a pastime or your livelihood.

- Whether the activity is carried out in a businesslike manner and the taxpayer maintains complete and accurate books and records.
- Whether the time and effort the taxpayer puts into the activity shows they intend to make it profitable.
- Whether they depend on income from the activity for their livelihood.
- Whether any losses are due to circumstances beyond the taxpayer's control or are normal for the startup phase of their type of business.
- Whether they change methods of operation to improve profitability.
- Whether the taxpayer and their advisors have the knowledge needed to carry out the activity as a successful business.
- Whether the taxpayer was successful in making a profit in similar activities in the past.
- Whether the activity makes a profit in some years and how much profit it makes.
- Whether the taxpayers can expect to make a future profit from the appreciation of the assets used in the activity.

Here's a fact to keep in mind. Do you know what defines a small business? Well, in 2025, it means a business making less than $47 million a year, according to the SBA

To satisfy the IRS's expectations for what constitutes a business, this ledger can help with the following:

Track Writing Time and Writing Business Time

While you know that you should keep track of your expenses, you also need to keep track of how much time you are investing in your writing business. See the second bullet in the list above. Let's pretend you didn't make any money with your writing (kind of easy to do), but you invested a lot of your money into your writing venture and would like to deduct those expenses. The IRS may ask you to prove that you actually worked at writing and made a serious go at it. Tracking how much time you worked in your writing business is your proof.

Track Submissions, Queries, Applications, and Writing Related Work

Same principle. The IRS may ask for proof that you attempted to make money from your writing. Again, see the second bullet in the list. Tracking your submissions and other writing related activities, like

trying to acquire an agent, is your proof that you are seriously attempting to make writing a career. Publication isn't the only way to prove you're a writer.

Track Income

Income made from just about anything is taxable. You must abide by what is legal. Consult a tax professional. There are different types of income. The income from an employer is documented with a W-2. The income from hired or contracted or self-employed work is documented with a 1099. For example, if you publish a book on Amazon, you will need to download your 1099 from your Amazon KDP account (no, they don't mail this to you). You will need to do this with all the platforms you publish on. There's also income from direct sales you personally make. For example, if you sell books or other items at a book fair or convention, you are expected to include those sales in your income.

Track Expenses

Money you invest in your writing business **might** be deductible from your taxes. It is crucial to consult the tax information for the year you are filing your taxes. Tax law changes all the time. Per diem rates, mileage rates, etc. constantly change. And remember that expenses must be *ordinary and necessary*. Keep track of every penny you spend. Record every expense in this tracker. Don't discount any expense. Let your tax professional make that call.

Make sure you do not double account or double deduct.
Items like sales tax will appear in multiple sections of this tracker.

Keep Those Receipts and Create a Filing System

Find a method to save those physical receipts. A binder, folder, file system, plastic container. Whatever your style may be. Join the rewards programs of your favorite stores because many keep track of your purchases (in-store and online) in your account. Accessing receipts today is much easier than in the past.

This tracker is divided into 6 sections:

1) **Track Your Work Time**: Writing and Writing Business
2) **Track Your Writing Related Work**: Submissions, Acceptances, Grants, Lectures, etc.
3) **Track Your Income**: Book sales, Teaching, Stipends, etc.
4) **Track Your Expenses**: A list of what can be expensed can be found in this document: https://www.irs.gov/forms-pubs/guide-to-business-expense-resources.
5) **Taxes:** Help you prepare for filing your taxes. **Please consult a tax professional.**
6) **Resources**

DID YOU KNOW?

According to WWM's survey, Authors with 25+ books **have a** median income of $3,000/month. And of those with 25+ books, 40%+ **of them earn** $5,000+/month

Sections

- **Section 1: Track Your Work Time: Writing and Writing Business** – This is proof that you are investing time in your business.

- **Section 2: Track Your Work** – Submissions; Queries to publishers and agents; Applications to writing programs or grants. Basically, if you sent something off to someone related to writing work, document it.

- **Section 3: Track Your Income** – Royalties; One-time payments; Selling copies on your own. Maybe you received a speaking fee. Or perhaps you did some teaching on one of the many teaching platforms. If you earned money from your writing business, document it.

- **Section 4: Track Your Expenses** – While every effort was made to include as many expense categories as possible, you might have your own unique ones. Many of the tables contain extra columns for your use. In addition, you will find many blank tables for you to customize. Don't be timid about customizing this workbook.

- **Section 5: Taxes** – Please use the IRS website and a tax professional. The tables in this section are just reminders of some of the information you need to document. Use a tax professional or accountant to learn how to be a self-employed taxpayer.

- **Section 6: Resources** – Some suggestions for helping you with what can be the confusing maze of taxes. Note: Websites come and go. Many websites don't get updated. Some become outdated. Check the year of your source. Check the creator of your source. Fact check the facts.

A Note on Content

This tracker is created for writers and the business of writing. Too many accounting ledgers and workbooks for writers aren't comprehensive enough or provide the space to document everything associated with your writing business. You will find that the tables are for the most part quite large, and the font size doesn't require a magnifying glass.

Tables

No ledger system is perfect. Needs and styles differ from person to person. This tracker is designed for you to customize. You will find:

- Tables with extra rows and columns.
- Blank tables.
- Wide margins for expanding tables, taking notes, and creating keys.
- If you need more pages, make copies for your use only.
- Whiteout headings and rename them to your liking.
- Get some colored pencils and color code your tables.
- Use stickers and tabs.

This is your tracker so make it your own.

Digital Version

A PDF version of this tracker is available for purchase at https://www.esmagill.com/nonfiction.

Tools to Use with this Tracker

Ruler, pens, pencils, color pencils, tape, correction tape, correction fluid, washi tape, stickers, glue stick, tape, tabs, etc. This is your tracker. Customize it.

Keep Up-to-Date Records

Make every effort to record daily. The next best is weekly and then monthly. Quarterly? You're pushing it. At the end of the year or start of the next? It's never too late, but it's better to start early in the year.

Create a basket for your receipts and place this Tracker with it. All you need to do then is schedule a record-keeping date, pick up the whole basket, and find a cozy nook to do your accounting. Make yourself a nice of cup tea, too. Accounting never sounded so fun.

May you have a successful writing year!

Don't rely on your memory. Keep records and receipts.
Document everything.
Consult a Tax Professional.
And do your research on the IRS website.

Section 1

TRACK YOUR WORK TIME

Writing

&

Writing Business

Document Time Spent Writing & Doing Writing Business

Writing Time | **JANUARY** | **Quarter 1**

Month	Monday	Tuesday	Wednesday	Thursday	Friday	Saturday	Sunday	Total Time	
Week 1									
Week 2									
Week 3									
Week 4									
Week 5									
Notes						Total Monthly Time			

Writing Business

Month	Monday	Tuesday	Wednesday	Thursday	Friday	Saturday	Sunday	Total Time	
Week 1									
Week 2									
Week 3									
Week 4									
Week 5									
Notes						Total Monthly Time			

Writing Time **FEBRUARY** **Quarter 1**

Month	Monday	Tuesday	Wednesday	Thursday	Friday	Saturday	Sunday	Total Time	
Week 1									
Week 2									
Week 3									
Week 4									
Week 5									
Notes						Total Monthly Time			

Writing Business

Month	Monday	Tuesday	Wednesday	Thursday	Friday	Saturday	Sunday	Total Time	
Week 1									
Week 2									
Week 3									
Week 4									
Week 5									
Notes						Total Monthly Time			

Writing Time **MARCH** **Quarter 1**

Month	Monday	Tuesday	Wednesday	Thursday	Friday	Saturday	Sunday	Total Time	
Week 1									
Week 2									
Week 3									
Week 4									
Week 5									
Notes						Total Monthly Time			

Writing Business

Month	Monday	Tuesday	Wednesday	Thursday	Friday	Saturday	Sunday	Total Time	
Week 1									
Week 2									
Week 3									
Week 4									
Week 5									
Notes						Total Monthly Time			

Writing Time **APRIL** **Quarter 2**

Month	Monday	Tuesday	Wednesday	Thursday	Friday	Saturday	Sunday	Total Time	
Week 1									
Week 2									
Week 3									
Week 4									
Week 5									
Notes						Total Monthly Time			

Writing Business

Month	Monday	Tuesday	Wednesday	Thursday	Friday	Saturday	Sunday	Total Time	
Week 1									
Week 2									
Week 3									
Week 4									
Week 5									
Notes						Total Monthly Time			

Writing Time **MAY** **Quarter 2**

Month	Monday	Tuesday	Wednesday	Thursday	Friday	Saturday	Sunday	Total Time	
Week 1									
Week 2									
Week 3									
Week 4									
Week 5									
Notes						Total Monthly Time			

Writing Business

Month	Monday	Tuesday	Wednesday	Thursday	Friday	Saturday	Sunday	Total Time	
Week 1									
Week 2									
Week 3									
Week 4									
Week 5									
Notes						Total Monthly Time			

Writing Time **JUNE** **Quarter 2**

Month	Monday	Tuesday	Wednesday	Thursday	Friday	Saturday	Sunday	Total Time	
Week 1									
Week 2									
Week 3									
Week 4									
Week 5									
Notes						Total Monthly Time			

Writing Business

Month	Monday	Tuesday	Wednesday	Thursday	Friday	Saturday	Sunday	Total Time	
Week 1									
Week 2									
Week 3									
Week 4									
Week 5									
Notes						Total Monthly Time			

Writing Time **JULY** **Quarter 3**

Month	Monday	Tuesday	Wednesday	Thursday	Friday	Saturday	Sunday	Total Time	
Week 1									
Week 2									
Week 3									
Week 4									
Week 5									
Notes						Total Monthly Time			

Writing Business

Month	Monday	Tuesday	Wednesday	Thursday	Friday	Saturday	Sunday	Total Time	
Week 1									
Week 2									
Week 3									
Week 4									
Week 5									
Notes						Total Monthly Time			

Writing Time **AUGUST** **Quarter 3**

Month	Monday	Tuesday	Wednesday	Thursday	Friday	Saturday	Sunday	Total Time	
Week 1									
Week 2									
Week 3									
Week 4									
Week 5									
Notes						Total Monthly Time			

Writing Business

Month	Monday	Tuesday	Wednesday	Thursday	Friday	Saturday	Sunday	Total Time	
Week 1									
Week 2									
Week 3									
Week 4									
Week 5									
Notes						Total Monthly Time			

Writing Time **SEPTEMBER** **Quarter 3**

Month	Monday	Tuesday	Wednesday	Thursday	Friday	Saturday	Sunday	Total Time	
Week 1									
Week 2									
Week 3									
Week 4									
Week 5									
Notes						Total Monthly Time			

Writing Business

Month	Monday	Tuesday	Wednesday	Thursday	Friday	Saturday	Sunday	Total Time	
Week 1									
Week 2									
Week 3									
Week 4									
Week 5									
Notes						Total Monthly Time			

Writing Time **OCTOBER** **Quarter 4**

Month	Monday	Tuesday	Wednesday	Thursday	Friday	Saturday	Sunday	Total Time	
Week 1									
Week 2									
Week 3									
Week 4									
Week 5									
Notes						Total Monthly Time			

Writing Business

Month	Monday	Tuesday	Wednesday	Thursday	Friday	Saturday	Sunday	Total Time	
Week 1									
Week 2									
Week 3									
Week 4									
Week 5									
Notes						Total Monthly Time			

Writing Time **NOVEMBER** **Quarter 4**

Month	Monday	Tuesday	Wednesday	Thursday	Friday	Saturday	Sunday	Total Time	
Week 1									
Week 2									
Week 3									
Week 4									
Week 5									
Notes						Total Monthly Time			

Writing Business

Month	Monday	Tuesday	Wednesday	Thursday	Friday	Saturday	Sunday	Total Time	
Week 1									
Week 2									
Week 3									
Week 4									
Week 5									
Notes						Total Monthly Time			

Writing Time

DECEMBER

Quarter 4

Month	Monday	Tuesday	Wednesday	Thursday	Friday	Saturday	Sunday	Total Time	
Week 1									
Week 2									
Week 3									
Week 4									
Week 5									
Notes						Total Monthly Time			

Writing Business

Month	Monday	Tuesday	Wednesday	Thursday	Friday	Saturday	Sunday	Total Time	
Week 1									
Week 2									
Week 3									
Week 4									
Week 5									
Notes						Total Monthly Time			

End of the Year Time Documentation: Writing & Writing Business

Time: Writing

Quarter 1	Quarter 2	Quarter 3	Quarter 4	Total
Total	Total	Total	Total	Total

Time: Writing Business

Quarter 1	Quarter 2	Quarter 3	Quarter 4	Total
Total	Total	Total	Total	Total

Total Time: All Writing

Quarter 1	Quarter 2	Quarter 3	Quarter 4	Total
Total	Total	Total	Total	Total

Section 2

DOCUMENT YOUR WRITING WORK & PROJECTS

Projects
Submissions
Queries
Contests
Applications
Jobs
Positions
and
All Other Writing Activities

Document Short Projects

Short Project Examples: Articles, Short Stories, Novellas, Poems, Reader Magnets, Other Projects

Title		Submission Date	Acceptance/Rejection Date
Submitted To			
Type	Publication Date		Payment/Royalty
Notes			

Title		Submission Date	Acceptance/Rejection Date
Submitted To			
Type	Publication Date		Payment/Royalty
Notes			

Title		Submission Date	Acceptance/Rejection Date
Submitted To			
Type	Publication Date		Payment/Royalty
Notes			

Title		Submission Date	Acceptance/Rejection Date
Submitted To			
Type	Publication Date		Payment/Royalty
Notes			

Title		Submission Date	Acceptance/Rejection Date
Submitted To			
Type	Publication Date		Payment/Royalty
Notes			

Title		Submission Date	Acceptance/Rejection Date
Submitted To			
Type	Publication Date		Payment/Royalty
Notes			

Document Long Projects

Long Project Examples: Novels, Nonfiction Books, Anthologies, Collections, Comics, Graphic Novels, Picture Books, Audiobooks, Reader Magnets, Other Longer Works (Document all work even if not published.)

Title		**Submission Date**	**Acceptance/Rejection Date**
Submitted To			
Type	**Publication Date**		**Payment/Royalty**
Notes			

Title		**Submission Date**	**Acceptance/Rejection Date**
Submitted To			
Type	**Publication Date**		**Payment/Royalty**
Notes			

Title		**Submission Date**	**Acceptance/Rejection Date**
Submitted To			
Type	**Publication Date**		**Payment/Royalty**
Notes			

Title		Submission Date	Acceptance/Rejection Date
Submitted To			
Type	Publication Date		Payment/Royalty
Notes			

Title		Submission Date	Acceptance/Rejection Date
Submitted To			
Type	Publication Date		Payment/Royalty
Notes			

Title		Submission Date	Acceptance/Rejection Date
Submitted To			
Type	Publication Date		Payment/Royalty
Notes			

Title		Submission Date	Acceptance/Rejection Date
Submitted To			
Type	Publication Date		Payment/Royalty
Notes			

Title		Submission Date	Acceptance/Rejection Date
Submitted To			
Type	Publication Date		Payment/Royalty
Notes			

Title		Submission Date	Acceptance/Rejection Date
Submitted To			
Type	Publication Date		Payment/Royalty
Notes			

Document Queries

Query Examples: Agents, Novels, Stories, Editors, Projects, Proposals, Other

Query Recipient	**Submission Date**
Purpose of Query	
	Acceptance/Rejection
Notes	

Query Recipient	**Submission Date**
Purpose of Query	
	Acceptance/Rejection
Notes	

Query Recipient	**Submission Date**
Purpose of Query	
	Acceptance/Rejection
Notes	

Query Recipient	Submission Date
Purpose of Query	
	Acceptance/Rejection
Notes	

Query Recipient	Submission Date
Purpose of Query	
	Acceptance/Rejection
Notes	

Query Recipient	Submission Date
Purpose of Query	
	Acceptance/Rejection
Notes	

Document Applications

Application Examples: Awards, Contests, Workshops, Grants, Internships, Residencies, Other

(Document any fees in Section 3 "Track Your Expenses" as well.)

Application for	**Submission Date**
Submitted To	**Fee**
Type	**Outcome**
Notes	

Application for	**Submission Date**
Submitted To	**Fee**
Type	**Outcome**
Notes	

Application for	**Submission Date**
Submitted To	**Fee**
Type	**Outcome**
Notes	

Application for	Submission Date
Submitted To	Fee
Type	Outcome
Notes	

Application for	Submission Date
Submitted To	Fee
Type	Outcome
Notes	

Application for	Submission Date
Submitted To	Fee
Type	Outcome
Notes	

Document Newsletters

Date	Type/ Platform	Title	Purpose	Stats

Document Videos/Vlogs/Podcasts

Date	Type/Platform	Title	Purpose	Stats

Document Interviews & Appearances

Date	Type	Purpose	Venue/Platform	

Document Other Writing Related Work

Date	Type	Purpose		

DOCUMENT SOCIAL MEDIA TIME SPENT ON WRITING

Your Social Media Platforms (List your social media.)									
Social Media									
Abb.									

Social Media Plan							
Social Media	Monday	Tuesday	Wednesday	Thursday	Friday	Saturday	Sunday

January – Q1

Month	Monday	Tuesday	Wednesday	Thursday	Friday	Saturday	Sunday	Total Time	
Week 1									
Week 2									
Week 3									
Week 4									
Week 5									
Notes									

February

Month	Monday	Tuesday	Wednesday	Thursday	Friday	Saturday	Sunday	Total Time	
Week 1									
Week 2									
Week 3									
Week 4									
Week 5									
Notes									

March

Month	Monday	Tuesday	Wednesday	Thursday	Friday	Saturday	Sunday	Total Time	
Week 1									
Week 2									
Week 3									
Week 4									
Week 5									
Notes									

April – Q2

Month	Monday	Tuesday	Wednesday	Thursday	Friday	Saturday	Sunday	Total Time	
Week 1									
Week 2									
Week 3									
Week 4									
Week 5									
Notes									

May

Month	Monday	Tuesday	Wednesday	Thursday	Friday	Saturday	Sunday	Total Time	
Week 1									
Week 2									
Week 3									
Week 4									
Week 5									
Notes									

June

Month	Monday	Tuesday	Wednesday	Thursday	Friday	Saturday	Sunday	Total Time	
Week 1									
Week 2									
Week 3									
Week 4									
Week 5									
Notes									

July - Q3

Month	Monday	Tuesday	Wednesday	Thursday	Friday	Saturday	Sunday	Total Time	
Week 1									
Week 2									
Week 3									
Week 4									
Week 5									
Notes									

August

Month	Monday	Tuesday	Wednesday	Thursday	Friday	Saturday	Sunday	Total Time	
Week 1									
Week 2									
Week 3									
Week 4									
Week 5									
Notes									

September

Month	Monday	Tuesday	Wednesday	Thursday	Friday	Saturday	Sunday	Total Time	
Week 1									
Week 2									
Week 3									
Week 4									
Week 5									
Notes									

October – Q4

Month	Monday	Tuesday	Wednesday	Thursday	Friday	Saturday	Sunday	Total Time	
Week 1									
Week 2									
Week 3									
Week 4									
Week 5									
Notes									

November

Month	Monday	Tuesday	Wednesday	Thursday	Friday	Saturday	Sunday	Total Time	
Week 1									
Week 2									
Week 3									
Week 4									
Week 5									
Notes									

December

Month	Monday	Tuesday	Wednesday	Thursday	Friday	Saturday	Sunday	Total Time	
Week 1									
Week 2									
Week 3									
Week 4									
Week 5									
Notes									

Total Time on Social Media

Quarter 1	Quarter 2	Quarter 3	Quarter 4	Total
Platform + Time	Platform + Time	Platform + Time	Platform + Time	Platform + Time
Total	Total	Total	Total	Total

Date				
Notes				

Section 3

TRACK YOUR INCOME

Payments
Royalties
Books Sold
Other Items Sold
Grants
Subscriptions
Memberships
Stipends
Teaching
& Other Writing Related Income

Make sure you do not double account or double deduct.
Items will appear in multiple sections of this tracker.

One Time Payment Or No Payment: short stories, magazine articles, books, projects, etc.

Date	Type	Title	Published by	Payment	

Notes	Total Payments

Sale of Real Items You Direct Sell: This includes items (books, mugs, shirts, etc.) sold at bookfairs, online, signings, etc. (Document sales tax you collect and must remit in Section 5 "Taxes.")

Date	Platform/ Location	Items	Cost of Item	(Fees)	(Sales Tax)	(Sales Tax: Indicate either *self remit or *sales platform remit)	Net Sales
TOTALS							

*Some sales platforms remit sales tax on your behalf. Find out if yours does or doesn't.

*Please see the Introduction, page 4, for a reminder about sales tax...and Nexus.

Sale of Real Items You Sell Online: This includes books and other physical items you sell through your website or personal store or a platform. (Document sales tax you collect and must remit in Section 5 "Taxes.")

Date	Platform/ Location	Items	Cost of Item	(Fees)	(Sales Tax)	(Sales Tax: Indicate either *self remit or *sales platform remit)	Net Sales
TOTALS							

Sale of Direct Digital Items: This includes e-books and audio you sell yourself through your website or personal store or a platform. (Document sales tax you collect and must remit in Section 5 "Taxes.")

(Also, some states don't place a sales tax on digital goods. Do your research.)

Date	Platform/ Location	Items	Cost of Item	(Fees)	(Sales Tax)	(Sales Tax: Indicate either *self remit or *sales platform remit)	Net Sales
			TOTALS				

Royalty Payments: books, audio, etc. You can track by Project or Platform. For example, you might document the royalties for each of your writing projects. Or you might document all the books you have on a particular platform.

Project/Platform

	Jan	Feb	Mar	Apr	May	June	July	Aug	Sept	Oct	Nov	Dec
Week												
Week												
Week												
Week												
Week												
Actual Month Totals												
Notes									Total			

Project/Platform

	Jan	Feb	Mar	Apr	May	June	July	Aug	Sept	Oct	Nov	Dec
Week												
Week												
Week												
Week												
Week												
Actual Month Totals												
Notes									Total			

Project/Platform

	Jan	Feb	Mar	Apr	May	June	July	Aug	Sept	Oct	Nov	Dec
Week												
Week												
Week												
Week												
Week												
Actual Month Totals												
Notes									Total			

Project/Platform

	Jan	Feb	Mar	Apr	May	June	July	Aug	Sept	Oct	Nov	Dec
Week												
Week												
Week												
Week												
Week												
Actual Month Totals												
Notes									Total			

Project/Platform

	Jan	Feb	Mar	Apr	May	June	July	Aug	Sept	Oct	Nov	Dec
Week												
Week												
Week												
Week												
Week												
Actual Month Totals												
Notes									Total			

Project/Platform

	Jan	Feb	Mar	Apr	May	June	July	Aug	Sept	Oct	Nov	Dec
Week												
Week												
Week												
Week												
Week												
Actual Month Totals												
Notes									Total			

Project/Platform

	Jan	Feb	Mar	Apr	May	June	July	Aug	Sept	Oct	Nov	Dec
Week												
Week												
Week												
Week												
Week												
Actual Month Totals												

Notes	Total

Project/Platform

	Jan	Feb	Mar	Apr	May	June	July	Aug	Sept	Oct	Nov	Dec
Week												
Week												
Week												
Week												
Week												
Actual Month Totals												

Notes	Total

Royalties Paid Yearly Total

Project/ Platform	Q1	Q2	Q3	Q4	Total
Total					
Notes					

Grants/Scholarships/Stipends/Other

Date	Type	Source	Amount	Notes
Total				

Courses/Workshops You Teach: Online or In-Person (Self-Employed/Not W-2 income.)

Date	Type	Source	Earnings	Notes
Notes:			**Total:**	

Subscriptions/Memberships: Sites where you have accounts for exclusive access for your paying fans. Blank columns are for you to customize. (Patreon, Substack, YouTube, etc.)

Platform:

Month				Earnings
January				
February				
March				
April				
May				
June				
July				
August				
Sept.				
October				
November				
December				
Notes			**Yearly Total**	

Sources of Earnings for the Year

Royalties/One Time Payments/Direct Sales/Subscriptions/Courses/ Other Income (not W-2 income)

Source	Goods/Services	Gross Earnings	Net Earnings	Notes

Earnings Gross Yearly Total	Earnings Net Yearly Total

Section 4

EXPENSES

A- Z Categories

Mostly Alphabetical
Some are grouped for convenience.

Make sure you do not double account or double deduct.
Items can appear in multiple sections of this tracker.

Advertising – Marketing – Promotion

Ads

Date	Project	Type of Ad			Cost
Notes				Total	

Promotions

Date	Project	Promotion Site			Cost
Notes				**Total**	

Marketing

Date	Project	Purpose			Cost
Notes				**Total**	

Advance Reader Copies (ARCS) / Proof Copies

Date	Title	Vendor/Source	Purpose	Cost
Total				

Banking

Date			
Notes			

Audio Recording Production

Audio Project 1	Date
Company/Platform	
Narrator	**Cost**
	Total Cost
Notes	

Audio Project 2	Date
Company/Platform	
Narrator	**Cost**
	Total Cost
Notes	

Audio Project 3	Date
Company/Platform	
Narrator	**Cost**
	Total Cost
Notes	

Audio Project 4	Date
Company/Platform	
Narrator	Cost
	Total Cost
Notes	

Audio Project 5	Date
Company/Platform	
Narrator	Cost
	Total Cost
Notes	

Notes	Total for All Audio Production

Books/Audio/Video

(Research; Books on Writing; Genre Writing; Market Research, etc.)

Date	Title	Purpose	Vendor	Total Cost

Notes	Total

Book Editing / Critique Services

Date					
Notes				Total	

Book Design & Production
(Detailed Method)

Book Project 1	Date
Cover	Cost
Formatting	Cost
Editing	Cost
	Total Cost
Notes	

Book Project 2	Date
Cover	Cost
Formatting	Cost
Editing	Cost
	Total Cost
Notes	

Book Project 3		Date
Cover		Cost
Formatting		Cost
Editing		Cost
	Total Cost	
Notes		

Book Project 4		Date
Cover		Cost
Formatting		Cost
Editing		Cost
	Total Cost	
Notes		

Book Project 5	Date
Cover	Cost
Formatting	Cost
Editing	Cost
	Total Cost
Notes	

Book Project 6	Date
Cover	Cost
Formatting	Cost
Editing	Cost
	Total Cost
Notes	

Notes	Total for All Book Production

Book Design & Production

(Simplified Method – but don't double account from detailed.)

Date	Project			Cost

Notes	Total

Business Meetings

Date	Purpose	Meals @ 50%		Total

Notes	Total

Date				

Notes

Cell Phone/Internet

Month	Phone % used business	Cost	Internet % used business	Cost
January				
February				
March				
April				
May				
June				
July				
August				
September				
October				
November				
December				
Total			**Total**	

Date				Total
Notes			**Total**	

Conferences/Workshops/Conventions/Book Events
(Local only. No overnight stays. Don't double account from Travel.)

Date	Event	Cost/ Fees	Daily Expenses	*Mileage/ Transportation	Total Cost

*Either record Mileage here OR in the Mileage Table. Just don't double account or double deduct.

Notes	Total

Contracted Help: Agent, Publicist, Manager, Marketing Company

Name/Company	Dates
Purpose	
Cost	Total
Notes	

Name/Company	Dates
Purpose	
Cost	Total
Notes	

Name/Company	Dates
Purpose	
Cost	Total
Notes	

Direct Sales

Date				

Notes

Date				

Notes

Date					
Notes				**Total**	

Fees

(Legal, Government, Business, Sales Tax Permits, Licenses, Incorporation)

Date	Type			Total
Notes			**Total**	

Date				

Health/Dental/Vision Insurance Self-Employed

(Not part of an employer's or government plan. Must consult IRS rules.)

Month					Total Cost
January					
January					
February					
February					
March					
March					
April					
April					
May					
May					
June					
June					
July					
July					
August					
August					
September					
September					
October					
October					
November					
November					
December					
December					
Totals					

Pension Plan Self-Employed

(Not part of an Employee Plan.)

Home Office

(Two methods to calculate – Standard and Actual)

https://www.irs.gov/

1) Standard/Simplified Method:

First calculate the square footage of your office/portion of home (maximum of 300 sq. ft.).

____

Next multiply the square footage by the current IRS Rate of (________)

________________________(sq. footage) X ____________________(IRS Rate)

= ___________________________________ (deductible total)

Or

2) Actual Expense Method: Very specific rules and criteria for this method. Please consult a tax professional or the IRS. If you are a homeowner, there are long term consequences if you choose this method.

Book Inventory: For businesses with low gross receipts (around $25M or less), you are allowed to expense book inventory as supplies. Treat inventory purchases as an expense and deduct the cost in the year the inventory was purchased.

Date	Item Purchased	Vendor	Quantity	Total Cost		Quantity of Items at Year's End	Notes

Total Cost	Notes:

ISBNs

Date	Quantity	ISBNs	Note	Cost
Total Cost				

Barcodes

(Many sales platforms use their own, so you don't have to purchase these – unless you have your own reason like direct selling.)

Date	Quantity	Barcodes	Note	Cost
Total Cost				

Mileage/Auto Expenses

Two Ways to Calculate: Standard or Actual

https://www.irs.gov

STANDARD METHOD

First, calculate your mileage for the year: ____________________

(See your Mileage Table.)

Next, find the current IRS mileage rate for the year: ________________

Then multiply your mileage by the mileage rate

__________________ X __________________ = ________________(deduction)

Parking & Tolls

Date	Destination/Purpose	Toll	Parking	Cost
Notes		Total	Total	Total Toll/Parking

Mileage + Parking & Tolls =	Total Deduction

Mileage

Trips to the store for writing supplies, bookstores, local events, travel, library, etc.
Do not double account from other tables, like Conferences or Travel.
*Odometer readings for each trip are not required by the IRS.
You only need to record the odometer reading at the start of the year and the end of the year.

Odometer Start of the Year______________________________

Odometer End of the Year ______________________________

MILEAGE TABLE

Date	Destination	Purpose	Miles
Notes		**Total Miles**	

OR 2) Actual Car Expense Method:

(There are specific guidelines and rules. Consult a trusted tax source.)

OFFICE EQUIMPENT & FURNISHINGS

Date	Vendor	Item		Total

Note	Total

OFFICE ELECTRONICS

Date	Vendor	Item		Total

Note	Total

OFFICE SUPPLIES

Date	Vendor	Item		Total
			Total	

PERIODICALS
(magazines, newsletters, journals related to writing)

Purchase Date	Title	Purpose	Cost		Renewal Date
Notes			Total		

POSTAGE/MAILING

Date	USPS/Other Company	Item	Purpose	Cost

Notes	Total

PROFESSIONAL DEVELOPMENT

(Courses, Workshops – Don't double account from other tables.)

Date	Course Title	Purpose	Source	Cost
Notes			Total	

PROFESSIONAL ORGANIZATIONS

Date	Organization	Cost/Dues	Renewal Date	
Notes			, **Total**	

Date				
Notes			**Total**	

PROMOTIONAL MATERIALS

(business cards, bookmarks, postcards, pens, banners, giveaways)

Date	Vendor	Item	Purpose	Cost

Notes	**Total**

SOFTWARE/APPS
(one-time or lifetime purchase)

Date	Title	Purpose	One-time or Lifetime	Cost

Notes	Total

SOFTWARE/APPS
(monthly subscriptions)

Start Date	Title	Purpose	Cost	Renewal Date	Password
Notes			Total		

SOFTWARE/APPS
(yearly subscriptions)

Start Date	Title	Purpose	Cost	Renewal Date	Password

Notes	Total

TRAVEL FOR BUSINESS

Overnight trips for conventions; research trips; book tours; conferences, etc.
See https://www.irs.gov/taxtopics/tc511 for specifics regarding lodging, per diems, etc.
Per diem rates and rules are different for employees versus the self-employed.
Use the current tax year's tax guidelines and rates. Do your research.

https://www.irs.gov/pub/irs-pdf/p463.pdf

TRAVEL 1:

Date	**Event**	
Location	**Ticket Price**	
Purpose		

Transportation				
Date	Mode	Purpose	Mileage*	Cost
Notes			**Total**	

*If you are driving, leave mileage in this chart. Just don't double account.

Lodging			
Date	Type/Location		Cost
Notes		**Total**	

Misc. Expenses (Verify what is deductible.)	
Notes	**Total**

Meals: Itemize meals **or** use per diem. Research travel expense rules. They change all the time. There's a rule about deductions on travel days as well.

Meals Itemize			
Day 1	Day 2	Day 3	Day 4
Meal 1	Meal 1	Meal 1	Meal 1
Meal 2	Meal 2	Meal 2	Meal 2
Meal 3	Meal 3	Meal 3	Meal 3
Misc.	Misc.	Misc.	Misc.
(or) Meals Per Diem (research current rate for location)			
Per Diem	Per Diem	Per Diem	Per Diem
Notes		**Total**	

TOTAL COST		
Cost of Event		
Transportation		
Housing		
Meals		
Misc.		
TOTAL		

TRAVEL 2:

Date	Event		
Location		Ticket Price	
Purpose			

Transportation

Date	Mode	Purpose	Mileage* (if driving)	Cost
Notes			Total	

Lodging

Date	Type/Location		Cost
Notes		Total	

Misc. Expenses

Notes			Total	

Meals Itemize			
Day 1	Day 2	Day 3	Day 4
Meal 1	Meal 1	Meal 1	Meal 1
Meal 2	Meal 2	Meal 2	Meal 2
Meal 3	Meal 3	Meal 3	Meal 3
Misc.	Misc.	Misc.	Misc.
(or) Meals Per Diem			
Per Diem	Per Diem	Per Diem	Per Diem
Notes		Total Cost	

TOTAL COST		
Cost of Event		
Transportation		
Housing		
Meals		
Misc.		
TOTAL		

TRAVEL 3:

Date	Event	
Location	Ticket Price	
Purpose		

Transportation				
Date	Mode	Purpose	Mileage* (if driving)	Cost
Notes			Total	

Lodging			
Date	Type/Location		Cost
Notes		Total	

Misc. Expenses				
Notes			Total	

Meals Itemize			
Day 1	Day 2	Day 3	Day 4
Meal 1	Meal 1	Meal 1	Meal 1
Meal 2	Meal 2	Meal 2	Meal 2
Meal 3	Meal 3	Meal 3	Meal 3
Misc.	Misc.	Misc.	Misc.
(or) Meals Per Diem			
Per Diem	Per Diem	Per Diem	Per Diem
Notes		Total Cost	

TOTAL COST		
Cost of Event		
Transportation		
Housing		
Meals		
Misc.		
TOTAL		

Website/Web Hosting/Web Domains
(Simple method)

Date	Provider/Service	Type	Cost	Renewal Date
Notes			Total Cost	

WEBSITE/WEB HOSTING/WEB DOMAINS

(Detailed but don't double account from Simple method.)

Date			
Purpose			
Notes			Total Cost

Date			
Purpose			
Notes			Total Cost

Date			
Purpose			
Notes			Total Cost

Section 5

TAXES

Disclaimer: This workbook does not give any advice about taxes or related topics. The author is not a tax expert. Use a professional accountant, lawyer, or tax advisor for all your tax needs. This workbook is for the sole purpose of recording information only.

Consult the Internal Revenue Service for accurate information.

https://www.irs.gov/businesses/small-businesses-self-employed

Make sure you do not double account or double deduct.
Items can appear in multiple sections of this tracker.

What's the difference between a W-2 and a 1099? Scan here.

PART 1: Document Your Earnings

Document Your Earnings - W-2s
(You as an employee)

Date	Sources		W-2 Earnings

*I hope you don't need to have this many jobs to support your writing business.

Notes	Total W-2 Earnings

Document Your Earnings - 1099s

(as self-employed / independent contractor)

https://www.irs.gov/businesses/small-businesses-self-employed

For many of the platforms, publishing and payment, (such as KDP/Amazon) you must print your own 1099 from your account. These will not be mailed or emailed to you. Some publishing platforms (such as IngramSpark) do not issue 1099s, so this means you need to check your account on these sites for your sales. Some platforms only issue a 1099 when you meet a certain sales threshold, but you will still need to report your sales on your tax return. If you publish wide or use various payment apps, keep track of these platforms.

If the platform does not issue you a 1099, then document your earnings in the next table.

Date	Source		1099 Earnings

Notes	1099 Earnings Total

Document Your Earnings – Platforms That Don't Issue 1099s

(See the explanation on the previous page.)

(as self-employed / independent contractor)

https://www.irs.gov/businesses/small-businesses-self-employed

Some publishing platforms (such as IngramSpark) do not issue 1099s, so this means you need to check your account on these sites for your sales.

If the platform does not issue you a 1099, then document your earnings in this table.

Date	Source		Earnings

Notes	1099s Earnings Total

Document Other Earnings

(Income not covered by a 1099: workshops taught, speaking engagements, etc.)

Consult Section 3 "Income" of this Workbook.

https://www.irs.gov/businesses/small-businesses-self-employed

Don't double account or deduct.

Type	Source		Earnings
Other			
Other			

Notes	Other Earnings Total

Document Direct Sales Earnings

https://www.irs.gov/businesses/small-businesses-self-employed

Don't double account or deduct.

*Type	Source		Earnings
Direct Sales of Real Items in Person page 46			
Direct Sales of Real Items Sold Online page 47			
Direct Sales of Digital Items page 48			

Notes	Direct Sales Earnings Total

All Earnings

Consult Section 3 "Income" of this Workbook.

How you choose to do your accounting is up to you. Be clear. Be careful. Don't double account or deduct.

Type	Source	Notes	Earnings Total
All W-2s Page 109			
All 1099s Page 110			
Platforms That Don't Issue 1099s Page 111			
Other Earnings See Section 112			
*Direct Sales	Source	Notes	Total
Real Items Direct Sales in Person page 113			
Direct Sales Online page 113			
Direct Sales Digital Items page 11348			
Notes			All Earnings Total

PART 2: Taxes

Self-Employment Tax

https://www.irs.gov/businesses/small-businesses-self-employed/self-employment-tax-social-security-and-medicare-taxes#2

Quarter Date	Net Earnings	Self-Employment Tax (See current rate.)	Total
Notes			**Yearly Total**

Estimated Quarterly Tax Payments for the Self-Employed
There are rules about when you need to start paying taxes quarterly. Check the Income threshold.
Remember, your Income is Gross minus Deductions. This will be your Net income.
Contact a Tax Professional.

Quarter 1

Date Paid	Previous Year's Income	Estimated Quarterly Tax Payment	Note

Quarter 2

Date Paid	Previous Year's Income	Estimated Quarterly Tax Payment	Note

Quarter 3

Date Paid	Previous Year's Income	Estimated Quarterly Tax Payment	Note

Quarter 4

Date Paid	Previous Year's Income	Estimated Quarterly Tax Payment	Note

For Year ______________

Date Paid	**Previous Year's Earnings Total**	**Estimated Quarterly Tax Payments Total**	

1099s You Need to Issue for Hired/Contracted Work

This is for your contracted workers who are U.S. taxpayers. Consult a Tax Professional.
https://www.irs.gov/businesses/small-businesses-self-employed/reporting-payments-to-independent-contractors

Date	Individual Or Company	Purpose	Amount	

Notes

Sales Tax You Collected and Are Responsible for Remitting.

Some publishing and payment platforms do not remit sales tax on your behalf. This becomes your responsibility. Consult a Tax Professional.

https://stripe.com/guides/how-to-file-sales-tax-us

You will need to remit sales tax (on products you direct sold) for the state in which you reside; this is your home state nexus.

Do you need to remit any payments directly to any other state in which you have nexus? (*If you do, then you won't be using this ledger because you'll be making enough money to pay an accountant.)

Use this table to keep track of sales tax filing dates and remittances so that you don't miss deadlines.

Don't use this table if the sales tax has been remitted by a platform on your behalf.

Date	Event		Sales Tax Collected	Filing Date	Date Paid

Notes

Other Tax Considerations

Quarter 1

Quarter 2

Quarter 3

Quarter 4

PART 3: Schedule C & Deductions

Schedule C

The following pages will help you complete Schedule C for your writing business.

<u>Consult the IRS website for correct information.</u>

https://www.irs.gov/forms-pubs

Find updated directions for your tax year.

<u>Please Consult a Tax Professional.</u>

Possible Tax Deductions for the Self-Employed Writer

Use the information from this Tracker to complete this worksheet.
Reference Section 4 "Expenses" to complete.

Consult a tax professional to determine what is deductible.
Consult a tax professional to complete your return.

Book Design & Production	Audiobook Design & Production
$____________Book 1	$____________Audiobook1
$____________Book 2	$____________Audiobook 2
$____________Book 3	$____________Audiobook 3
$____________Book 4	$____________Audiobook4
*And/Or Itemized Costs	*And/Or Itemized Costs
$____________Proof Copies/ARCS	$____________Narrators
$____________Covers	$____________Editing
$____________Editing	$____________Production
$____________ISBN Purchase	$____________Covers
$____________	$____________Inventory
$____________	$____________
$____________	$____________
$____________	$____________
$____________	$____________
$____________	$____________
*Don't double account between book total and itemized.	*Don't double account between audiobook total and itemized.
Publishing Expenses Total $________________	**Publishing Expenses Total** $________________

Car Usage Expenses	Office Space Expenses
Method 1 Standard/Simplified Method $________ (See page 85.) OR Method 2 Actual/Itemized $________	Home Office Space Standard/Simplified $________ (See page 82.) OR Office Actual/Itemized $________
Vehicle Usage Expenses Total $____________	Office Space Expenses Total $____________

Contracted Labor Expenses	Legal/Professional Expenses
$________Agent $________Publicist $________Book Cover Artist/Design $________Book Editors $________Audio Producer $________Audio Cover Design $________Coach $________Assistant $________ $________ $________ $________	$________Licenses $________Sales Tax Permits $________Copyright Fees $________Trademark Fees $________Legal Fees $________ISBNs $________Attorney $________Bank Fees $________ $________ $________
Contracted Labor Expenses Total $____________	Taxes/Legal Matters Expenses Total $____________

Office/Business Expenses	Business Travel Expenses
$__________Office Supplies	$__________Travel 1
$__________Office Equipment	$__________Travel 2
$__________Furnishings	$__________Travel 3
$__________Office Computer	$__________Travel 4
$__________Office Electronics	OR
$__________Equipment Repair	$__________Mileage
$__________Internet	$__________Travel
$__________Monthly Apps	$__________Lodging
$__________Yearly Apps	$__________Meals per diem
$__________Life-time Apps	$__________Meals in full (less 50%)
$__________Software	$__________Wi-Fi Access
$__________Website Domains	$__________Use of Business Facilities
$__________Website Design	$__________Misc. Expenses
$__________Website Hosting	$__________Cost for Conferences
$__________Direct Sales	$__________Materials
$__________	$__________
$__________	$__________
$__________	$__________
$__________	$__________
$__________	$__________
$__________	$__________
Office Expenses Total $______________	Travel Expenses Total $______________ Travel less Meals Per Diem Total $______________ Travel less Meals in full (@50%) Total $______________

Postage	Printing
$______________	$______________

Benefits and Self-Employment Tax are not deducted on the Schedule C. Instead, this is reported on Schedule 1 of your 1040 tax return. Consult a tax professional.

Benefits	Self-Employment Tax
$__________Health Insurance $__________Dental Insurance $__________Vision Insurance $__________Pension Plan $__________ $__________ *As self-employed only. Not part of a company or other plan. Report on Schedule 1. You must meet certain criteria to claim this. Consult a tax pro.	**There is a formula for determining the SE Tax.** **Please visit https://www.irs.gov/businesses/small-businesses-self-employed/self-employment-tax-social-security-and-medicare-taxes**
Benefits Expenses Total $______________	**Total** $______________

Taxes	
$__________ $__________ $__________ $__________ $__________ $__________	$__________ $__________ $__________ $__________ $__________ $__________
Total $______________	**Total** $______________

Ads/Promos/Marketing Expenses	Professional/Development Expenses
$____________Advertising	$____________Local Seminars/Courses/ Workshops/Book Events
$____________Promotions	$____________Course/Seminar Materials
$____________Marketing Apps	$____________Journals/Periodicals/ Magazines
$____________Business Cards	$____________Books/Audio/Video for Research
$____________Promotional Materials	$____________Professional Organization Fees & Dues
$____________	$____________Union Fees
$____________	$____________Business Meetings
$____________	$____________Contests/Awards
$____________	$____________Meals in full (less 50%) for local business meetings
$____________	$____________
$____________	$____________
$____________	$____________
$____________	$____________
$____________	$____________
$____________	$____________
$____________	$____________
$____________	
$____________	
$____________	
Ads/Promos/Marketing Expenses Total $_______________	Professional Development Expenses Total $_______________

Worksheet that Correlates with the Schedule C
(Use the previous pages to complete.)

Expenses	Amount
Accounting	
Advertising/Marketing/Promotion	
Bank Charges	
Benefits Programs: health, dental, vision*	
Car Expenses (Standard or Actual)	
Contracted Labor	
Dues	
Insurance	
Interest	
Legal & Professional	
Office (Standard or Actual)	
Pension Plans*	
Postage	
Printing	
Repairs	
Supplies (all categories of Office)	
Taxes	
Taxes Self-Employment	
Taxes Sales – That you have collected and need to remit and are included in your Gross Earnings. If you've already deducted collected sales tax from your Gross, do not include here.	
Telephone	
Internet	
Travel Total (minus meals per diem)	
Meals Per Diem For Travel	
Meals in full (less 50%) for local business meetings	

Other	
Professional Development (all)	
Book Design & Production	
Audio Design & Production	
Total	

Other Deductions

Purchases Costing More than $2,500 Per Item* (Consult a Tax Professional.)

Date	Item	Cost	Notes

*Explained: https://bit.ly/4jonf2U

***Now take all this to your Tax Professional to prepare your taxes for filing.**

Resources

IRS Self-Employed Individual Tax Center

https://www.irs.gov/businesses/small-businesses-self-employed/self-employed-individuals-tax-center

Books:

Working for Yourself by NOLO, 11th Edition. ISBN-13: 978-1413325812

Other Resources:

https://www.thebalancecareers.com/taxes-and-the-book-author-2799907

https://blog.freelancersunion.org/2021/12/14/tax-planning-for-the-busy-freelancer

https://www.janefriedman.com/author-taxes/

https://www.nolo.com/legal-encyclopedia/tax-deductions-writers.html

https://www.tckpublishing.com/20-tax-deductions-for-writers/

https://www.toptaxdefenders.com/hs-fs/hub/139062/file-27719971-pdf/docs/333-tax-deductions.pdf

https://turbotax.intuit.com/tax-tips/self-employment-taxes/tax-tips-for-freelance-writers-and-self-published-authors/L1v0lGVru

https://www.writersdigest.com/get-published-sell-my-work/tax-advice-for-writers

***Tax law and tax forms are always changing. Check the date of all resources you consult.**

***Consult a tax professional.**

Made in the USA
Monee, IL
07 November 2026

67974633R00077